Science in a flash

Forces

Georgia Amson-Bradshaw

W
FRANKLIN WATTS
LONDON•SYDNEY

Franklin Watts
First published in Great Britain in 2017 by The Watts Publishing Group

Copyright © The Watts Publishing Group 2017

 Produced for Franklin Watts by
White-Thomson Publishing Ltd
www.wtpub.co.uk

Credits
Series Editor: Georgia Amson-Bradshaw
Series Designer: Rocket Design (East Anglia) Ltd

Images from Shutterstock.com: baltskars 5bl, Africa Studio 5br, Bas Nastassia 5tl, Chirtsova Natalia 5tr, enciktepstudio 4bl, Natalia Lebedinskaia 4br, Paul Fleet 8b, Brian A Jackson 8c, AngelPet 10br, Johan Swanepoel 11tr, supergenijalac 12bl, Barnaby Chambers 13r, ostill 13c, annalisa e marina durante 16b, Kostyantyn Ivanyshen 17t, Susii 21tr, Javier Brosch 23br, Sailorr 23c, Catmando 25c, Javier Brosch 25tl, dotshock 24c, Catalin Petolea 24b.
Illustrations by Steve Evans: 6, 7, 8br, 9c, 12t, 17br, 20c, 21b, 22b, 23b, 27br
All design elements from Shutterstock.

Every attempt has been made to clear copyright. Should there be any inadvertent omission please apply to the publisher for rectification.

HB ISBN 978 1 4451 5268 4
PB ISBN 978 1 4451 5269 1

Printed in China

MIX
Paper from
responsible sources
FSC® C104740
FSC
www.fsc.org

Franklin Watts
An imprint of
Hachette Children's Group
Part of The Watts Publishing Group
Carmelite House
50 Victoria Embankment
London EC4Y 0DZ

An Hachette UK Company
www.hachette.co.uk

www.franklinwatts.co.uk

In this book you'll see some words shown in **bold**. These are described on the glossary page at the back of the book .

Contents

WHAT IS A FORCE?

A force is a push or a pull.

Whenever something moves or changes shape, that is the result of a force pushing it or pulling it. There are lots of different kinds of force, and they can move things in different ways. Forces can be big or small, but nothing can move without a force making it happen.

Push me higher, minion!

Oh yeah, looking good.

PUSH!

Pushing something moves it away from you, such as when you push someone on a swing. You can apply a pushing force to something without moving it too, like when you lean against a wall. You push the wall, and the wall pushes you back.

PULL!

When you pull something, you move it towards you. You can pull open a drawer or pull your sock onto your foot. Pulling forces don't always move objects. **Gravity** is pulling on you even when you are still.

SQUASH!

By pressing or pushing on a soft object like a ball of plasticine, you can change its shape.

TWIST!

When we push or pull opposite sides of an object at the same time, we can twist it. This is how you twist open a jar or wring the water out of a flannel!

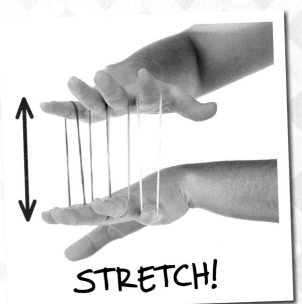

STRETCH!

Pulling forces can also cause things to change shape. Pulling on an elastic band makes it longer and thinner. Remove the pulling force by letting it go, and it pings back into shape.

MOVE!

Applying a force to an object can make it move or change direction. If an object is already moving, increasing force or adding another force can make it speed up or slow down.

Forces around us

Gravity, magnetism, friction, resistance, upthrust and tension are all forces around us.

Look around, and you will see examples of forces at work all the time. Forces can be very useful to us!

Upthrust

is a useful force that keeps objects like boats floating on water.

Air resistance

or **drag**, can be a drag when you want to go faster on your bike! But it is also the force that makes a parachute fall slowly and safely to the ground, or keeps a parasail up in the air.

Water resistance

is used when we paddle in a boat or on a board. It allows us to push against the water.

Riddle me this!

Even something lying still on the ground has several pushes and pulls acting on it. What do you think they are?

Answer on page 28.

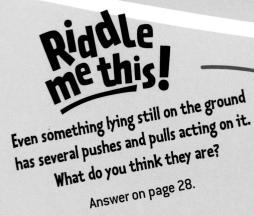

Magnetism

is a very useful force. It helps generate electricity in power plants, and is the force that makes compass needles point north.

Friction

is a force that slows things down. It is how brakes work.

Er, is the ski slope somewhere around here?

Tension

is used in lots of everyday objects. It makes the strings on a tennis racquet springy, so it pings the ball back quickly.

Gravity

causes objects to fall, and stops things from floating off. Without gravity, hitting a tennis ball would make it go zooming off into space!

WHAT IS GRAVITY?

Gravity is a force that tries to pull two objects towards each other.

Trip over, and you will fall down. Drop an object, and it will fall to the floor. The reason for this is gravity. But gravity does more than just cause people and things to fall. In fact, any two objects in the universe have this force between them, pulling them together.

Where did it all go wrong?

Gravity strikes again ...

Size matters

Most of the time the force of gravity between two objects is too small to notice. Gravity is strong when one of the objects is much, much bigger than the other.

Did you know?

The Earth is enormous compared to the people and objects on its surface – which is why its gravity pulls you (and everything else on Earth) down to it all the time.

Planetary pull

Gravity is also the force that keeps our solar system together. The Sun is much bigger than any of the planets, and so its gravitational pull keeps them circling around in **orbit**.

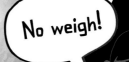

No weigh!

Big or heavy?

Gravity gives us **weight**. Our weight is the force of gravity pulling down on our **mass**. This means weight is a measurement of force, not of size.

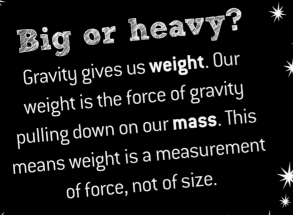

POP QUIZ!

Do you know how much you weigh? If you stood on the Moon and weighed yourself, would you:

a) **Weigh the same as you do on Earth?**
b) **Weigh less?**
c) **Weigh more?**

Answer on page 28.

FACT ATTACK

The gravitational pull of the Moon is the reason we have tides in the ocean. The water bulges out in the direction of the Moon, making it high tide in some places and low tide in others.

WHAT IS MAGNETISM?

Magnetism is a force that pushes or pulls some metal objects without touching them.

Magnetism is a mysterious-seeming force. Like gravity, it is a force that doesn't need objects to be touching each other to have an effect.

Magnetite

Making magnets

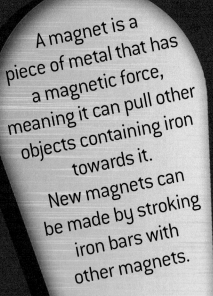

A magnet is a piece of metal that has a magnetic force, meaning it can pull other objects containing iron towards it.
New magnets can be made by stroking iron bars with other magnets.

FACT ATTACK

Super-strong magnets are used to separate iron and steel from other scrap at scrap yards.

North and south poles

All magnets have a magnetic **force field** around them. The magnetic force field is strongest at the two ends, called the **poles**. Each magnet has a north and a south pole. Scientists believe that the Earth has a big ball of iron in the centre, which creates a magnetic force field around the Earth.

Bar magnet

North Pole

Iron ball

South Pole

Ring magnet

Horseshoe magnet

EYE SPY!

How many magnets can you count?

Give it a go!

Find a bar magnet and collect some metallic objects from around your house, such as a paperclip, metal scourer, piece of aluminium foil, necklace chain, and so on.

Bring the magnet near each item in turn. Which objects stick to the magnet?

Why do some items stick, and others not? **Answer on page 28.**

All about friction

Friction is a force that stops objects sliding against each other.

When two objects rub together, their surfaces touch. Even surfaces that look smooth to our eyes are covered in very tiny lumps and dents, and when surfaces are slid across one another, these lumps catch and slow the objects down. This force is called **friction**, and it causes things to slow down and 'stick' together.

Types of friction

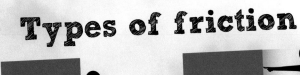

Static

Sliding

Easy!

There are two different kinds of friction, **static friction** and **sliding friction**. Static friction makes it difficult to move a stationary object. Sliding friction kicks in when something is moving. It slows down objects in motion.

Get a grip

As well as slowing us down, friction can help us get going. This is because static friction gives you 'grip'. Walking or driving would be impossible without friction: without it your foot would slip with every step, and a car tyre would spin against the road without going anywhere.

Riddle me this!

Can you think of any ways to reduce friction? This picture is a clue ...
Answer on page 28.

Slow down!

Brakes on bicycles use sliding friction. The brakes grip the moving wheel, and friction between the two surfaces slows the bike wheels down.

Give it a go!

Find two large, soft cover books of similar size. Interlace the pages a few at a time, so that the two books are 'woven' together.

Make sure to overlap them by several centimetres. When you have done all the pages, try to pull the books apart. They won't budge! The friction 'sticking' the pages together is just too strong.

What is air resistance?

Air resistance is a force that pushes against objects moving through air.

Think about riding your bike or scooter. The faster you go, the more you can feel the air rushing against you. This is air resistance, and it is affected by how fast an object is travelling, and how big it is.

A big push

Bigger objects have a bigger surface area for the air to push against, so they experience more resistance than smaller ones.

Faster is harder

The faster an object moves through the air, the more the air pushes back, or 'resists' it. A speedy motorcyclist will feel a bigger push than a slow cyclist. Air resistance is really a special type of friction, because the air is dragging at the object as it goes past.

Falling through air

It is difference in air resistance, NOT difference in gravity that is the reason some objects fall faster or slower to the ground. If you jumped out of a plane with no parachute, you'd hit the ground at high speed. A parachute creates a big, curved surface area that increases air resistance, slowing your fall to safe speeds.

I was aiming for a field but a busy road will have to do!

POP QUIZ!

What would fall faster, a flat piece of A4 paper, or a piece of A4 paper crumpled into a ball?

a) The flat piece would fall faster.
b) The crumpled ball will fall faster.
c) They would fall at the same speed.

Answer on page 28.

Sleek shapes

Air resistance can be reduced by **streamlining**. This means using smooth, pointed shapes. Streamlining is why sports cars have narrow, pointed shapes, rather than big, flat fronts like a truck.

What is water resistance?

Water resistance is a force that pushes back on objects moving through water.

If you've ever tried to run in a swimming pool, you'll know you can't go very fast! This is because water resistance is pushing at your legs, and slowing them right down.

A real drag

Water resistance is like air resistance, in that it is a special sort of friction or drag that gets stronger the faster and bigger an object is. But water resistance is stronger than air resistance because water is denser than air.

Om nom!

Quick fish

Because water resistance is more powerful than air resistance, streamlining is very important for animals who live in water. Sharks, who need to be able to swim fast to catch prey, have sleek bodies that let them cut through the water.

Yikes!

A. Flippers

C. Goggles

B. Rubber ring

POP QUIZ!

Water resistance can be useful, as well as an obstacle. Which of these objects uses water resistance as an advantage?

Answer on page 29.

Give it a go!

Test which shapes are more streamlined in this water resistance experiment.

You'll need a tray filled with water, some plasticine, and some chopsticks or pencils to use as a handles.

Using equal-sized pieces of plasticine, mould some different shapes around the ends of your sticks. Try a flat disc, a round ball, and a pointed lozenge shape.

Drag the shapes through the water. Which shapes feel the biggest push back from the water?

ALL ABOUT UPTHRUST

Upthrust is a force that pushes things upwards in water.

Have you ever tried lifting your friend up in the swimming pool? You probably found that it was much easier to lift them up in the water than when you are dry land! This is because of upthrust, which is a force that pushes things upwards in water and seems to make them weigh less.

Floating and sinking

Upthrust is the reason some things float and some things sink. When an object is put into water, it has to push some of the water out of the way in order to make space for itself.

Water weight

An object floats if it weighs less than the water it is trying to push out of the way. It sinks if it weighs more. An anchor weighs more than the water that takes up the same amount of space, so it sinks. The boat weighs less than the water that fills the same amount of space, so it floats.

WEIGHT

Riddle me this!

How could you change an object's shape but not its weight to make it sink or float?

Answer on page 29.

Light as air

Even heavy metal boats are mostly hollow — they contain a lot of air. This makes them lighter than the water they are trying to push out of the way.

Did you know?

Submarines use upthrust to sink and float. They have ballast tanks, which can contain air or water. When full of air, the sub is lighter so it floats. When the tanks fill with water, the sub gets heavier, and sinks.

To rise again after diving, compressed air is injected into the tanks, pushing the water out, and making the submarine light enough to float again.

UPTHRUST

ALL ABOUT ELASTICITY

Elastic forces are created in objects that have been stretched or squashed.

Some materials, such as rubber, are **elastic,** which means they can be stretched or squashed without breaking, and will ping back to their original shape afterwards. When an elastic material is stretched or squashed, a force develops.

Ping with a spring

By quickly releasing an object under tension or compression, you can ping things quite far and fast.

The force in a squashed material is called compression.

Squidge!

TWONG!

Think of a jack-in-the-box. When the lid is closed, the spring is squashed: it is under compression.

When the lid is opened, the spring is released, and BOING! The jack pops up quickly.

The force in a stretched material is called tension.

Awesome archery

A bow uses elastic tension to fire an arrow. Pulling backwards on the string creates tension in the bow. Releasing the string causes the bow to ping back into shape, pushing the arrow forwards at high speed.

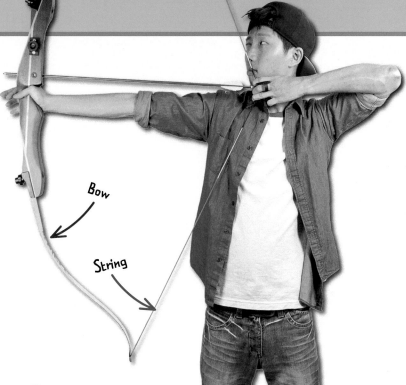

Bow

String

Give it a go!

See elastic tension in action by making your own mini bow and arrow.

You'll need a lolly stick, some dental floss, cotton buds, scissors, and a wide mug.

Soak your lolly stick in water for an hour until soft. Then, using the scissors, make small notches about 1cm from each end of the stick.

Leave the lolly stick to dry inside the rim of the mug, so it dries in a curved shape

When dry, tie some dental floss around the notches at one end. Pull the floss tight, and tie it off around the notches at the other end.

Pull the cotton off one end of several cotton buds. These are your arrows.

Hold one on the floss between your thumb and finger, pull back, and fire!

1. Lolly stick with notches

2. Lolly sticks drying inside mug

3. Finished lolly stick bow ready to fire!

Balanced and unbalanced forces

Balanced forces keep objects still, or moving at the same speed.

We know that forces are needed to get things moving, or to change their shape. But it's very rare for an object to be affected by only one force at a time, so if an object is still or moving at a steady speed, it means the forces acting on it are balanced.

Tug of war

Think of two evenly matched teams playing a game of tug of war. Even though both sides might be pulling as hard as they can, if both sides are pulling with exactly the same force, nobody goes anywhere. The teams stand still, despite the strong forces at work.

The forces acting on this crane are balanced.

We've been here for hours ...

22

Steady speed

Balanced forces acting on a moving object will keep it moving at a steady speed. If the forces become unbalanced, it will speed up, slow down or stop.

Normal force

Any object or person standing still is being acted on by at least two forces. We are constantly being pulled downwards by gravity, but the solid ground pushes back up with the same amount of force, so we don't sink into the floor. That push back is called **normal force**.

POP QUIZ!

Which two forces must be balanced to allow this duck to stay floating on the surface of the water?

Answer on page 29.

I can feel the force ... the normal force!

All about pressure

Eek!

Have you ever poked the tip of a sharp pencil into a rubber and made a little hole? It's easy enough to do. But it's not so easy to make a hole using the unsharpened end of a pencil – in fact, you probably can't do it. That's because of the way **pressure** works.

PINS AND PRESSURE

The same amount of pushing force will have a stronger or weaker effect, depending on how spread out or concentrated in one place it is. The bigger the area a pushing force is spread out over, the weaker it is. Pins work by concentrating the pushing force of your finger into a tiny area, so they can pierce a wall or pinboard.

POP QUIZ!

Which of these items deliberately increases the pressure of a pushing force, and which deliberately decreases it?
Answer on page 29.

A PAIR OF SNOW SHOES

A KITCHEN KNIFE

24

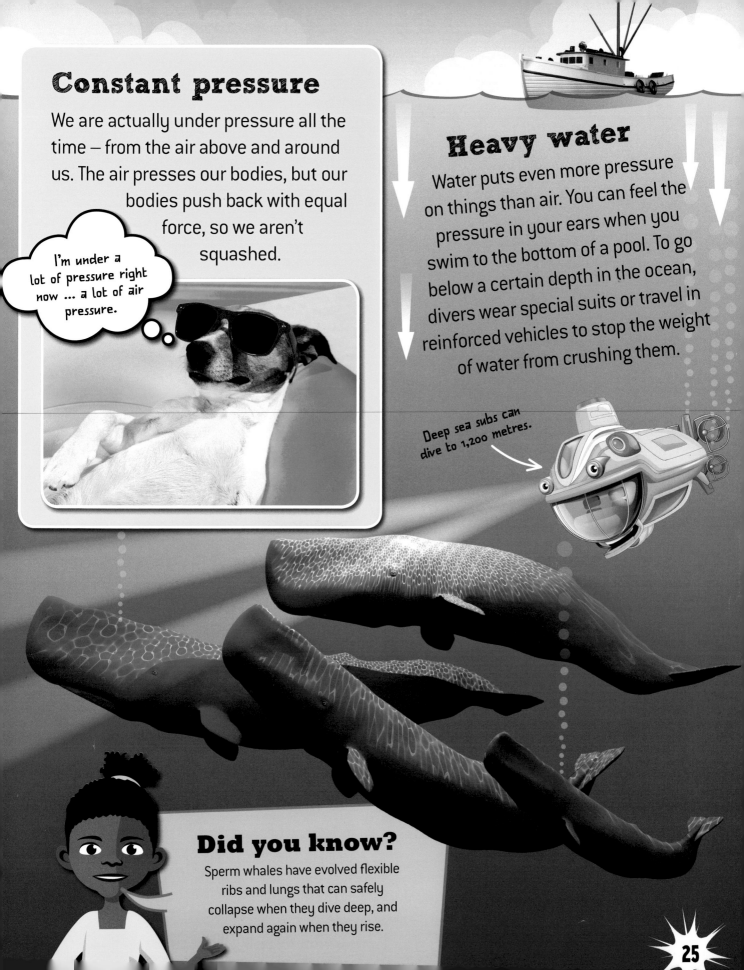

Constant pressure

We are actually under pressure all the time – from the air above and around us. The air presses our bodies, but our bodies push back with equal force, so we aren't squashed.

I'm under a lot of pressure right now ... a lot of air pressure.

Heavy water

Water puts even more pressure on things than air. You can feel the pressure in your ears when you swim to the bottom of a pool. To go below a certain depth in the ocean, divers wear special suits or travel in reinforced vehicles to stop the weight of water from crushing them.

Deep sea subs can dive to 1,200 metres.

Did you know?

Sperm whales have evolved flexible ribs and lungs that can safely collapse when they dive deep, and expand again when they rise.

MAKING FORCES BIGGER

We can use machines to make forces bigger, and do work for us.

When you hear the word 'machine' you probably think of a very complicated invention with lots of parts. But some are very simple. We use these simple machines to magnify forces, and make work easier.

Hard!

Easy!

Short distance

RAMPS

Long distance

HEAVY!

The simplest machine is the **ramp**. Lifting a heavy load straight upwards is difficult, but carrying it up a ramp is much easier. The trade-off is that you have to carry the load a longer distance.

HEAVY!

LEVERS

A **lever** is a beam that pivots around a fixed point. A see-saw is a lever. By moving the fixed point (called the **fulcrum**) closer to one end, you can change the amount of force needed to lift a load.

Easy!

HEAVY!

Fulcrum →

PULLEYS

A **pulley** is a machine made of one or more wheels and a rope. The rope attaches to the load at one end, loops round the wheels, and you pull on the opposite end. The more wheels, the more your pulling force is magnified.

Single pulley

Double pulley

A bit easier

Much easier

HEAVY!

HEAVY!

A single pulley (with one wheel) doesn't make your pulling force any bigger, but it is slightly easier to pull downwards with gravity than to pull straight up. A pulley with two wheels makes it twice as easy to lift the load, but you have to pull the rope further.

Give it a go!

Lift the shoe again by pulling downwards on the string. Can you feel a difference?

Make a single pulley using an empty thread spool, a skewer, some string and a weight, such as a shoe.

Slide the thread spool onto the skewer, and balance it between two chairs. Tie the string to the shoe.

First, try lifting the string and shoe directly upwards. Now try running the string over the top of the spool.

And the answer is...

Page 6

Riddle me this: An object lying on the ground is being pulled down by gravity, but the ground is pushing upwards with **normal force**. Read about normal force on page 23.

Page 9

Pop quiz: The answer is **b, you would weigh less**. This is because it is gravity pulling on your body that gives you weight, and there is less gravity on the Moon than on Earth.

Give it a go: Some metal items won't stick to the magnet because not every type of metal is magnetic. Only items containing the metals iron, nickel and cobalt will stick. Metals like tin or gold will not.

Page 11

Eye spy: There are are 11 magnets (including the electromagnet, the magnetite and the Earth's core).

Page 13

Riddle me this: One way to reduce friction is to cover surfaces with a slippery liquid, such as oil. This is called a lubricant. Another way to reduce friction is to make the surfaces that are touching smoother.

Page 15

Pop quiz: The answer is **b, the crumpled paper would fall faster**. This is because a flat sheet of paper has a larger surface area, so the air resistance pushing on it would be greater.

Pop quiz: The answer is **A, flippers**. The large surface area of a pair of flippers creates more water resistance for a swimmer to push against, and propel themselves through the water. A rubber ring does NOT use water resistance to keep swimmers afloat, it uses upthrust. Read about upthrust on page 18. The goggles do not affect water resistance.

Page 19

Riddle me this: One way to change something's shape to make it float is to make it hollow. For example, a solid ball of plasticine will sink, as it is heavier than the water that takes up the same space. But press the plasticine into a hollow bowl shape and it will float, because the space taken up by the plasticine and the air inside it is now less than the water it pushes out of the way.

Page 23

Pop quiz: Gravity and upthrust must be balanced to allow the duck to stay floating on the surface of the water.

Page 24

Pop quiz: The snow shoes work by decreasing pressure, and the knife works by increasing it. Snow shoes spread your weight over a larger surface area so that you don't sink down into the snow. A knife concentrates the pushing force of your arm into a very fine area to chop through food.

Glossary

Air resistance The pushing force of air on a moving object

Compression A force created when something is squeezed or squashed

Drag A type of friction from air or water that slows down moving objects

Elastic A material that is able to ping back into shape after it has been squashed or stretched

Force field An invisble area where a force has power

Friction A force created by two surfaces rubbing against one another

Fulcrum A fixed point that a lever moves around, such as the fixed middle point of a see-saw

Gravity A force that pulls objects together

Lever A simple machine that uses a beam moving round a fixed point to make lifting a load easier

Magnetism A force that attracts some types of metal

Magnetite A type of rock that contains iron and is a natural magnet

Mass The amount of matter, or stuff, an object or person is made of

Normal force The pushing force of the ground against an object resting on it

Orbit Move around another object in a circle

Poles The two ends of a magnet, where the magnetic force is strongest. The Earth also has magnetic poles

Pressure How spread out or concentrated a force is

Pulley A simple machine using wheels and rope that makes lifting a load easier

Ramp A simple machine that makes it easier to move a load upwards

Sliding friction Friction that slows an object when it is moving across a surface

Static friction Friction that grips an object in place and stops it from slipping

Streamlining Making an object more pointed and smooth so it can cut through air or water more easily

Tension A force created when something is stretched

Upthrust The upwards pushing force on an object in water

Water resistance The force pushing back on an object as it moves through water

Weight The force of an object pressing downwards because of the pull of gravity on its mass

Further reading

Heave: Forces and How They Move Things:
The Real Scientist
Peter Riley (Franklin Watts, 2012)

Forces: Project Science
Sally Hewitt (Franklin Watts, 2012)

Forces and Movement:
How Does Science Work
Carol Ballard (Wayland, 2014)

Electricity and Magnets: Mind Webs
Anna Claybourne (Wayland, 2014)

Forces and Magnets:
Moving Up With Science
Peter Riley (Watts, 2015)

Websites

www.msichicago.org/play/simplemachines/
Interactive games that test your understanding of forces and machines.

www.bbc.co.uk/education/topics/znmmn39
Video clips all about forces and motion.

www.exploratorium.edu/snacks/subject/mechanics-force-motion
Fun experiments to do at home.

www.explainthatstuff.com/motion.html
Detailed information about forces.

Every effort has been made by the Publishers to ensure that the websites in this book are suitable for children, that they are of the highest educational value, and that they contain no inappropriate or offensive material. However, because of the nature of the Internet, it is impossible to guarantee that the contents of these sites will not be altered. We strongly advise that Internet access is supervised by a responsible adult.

Index

Science in a Flash
Series contents lists

Earth and Space

- What is space? • All about stars and galaxies • What is the solar system? • All about the Sun • All about the Earth • How does the Earth move? • All about the Moon • How does the Moon move? • What is an eclipse? • All about the planets • What are asteroids and comets? • All about space travel

Living things

- What is a living thing? • How are living things grouped? • What is a habitat? • All about food chains • Producers, predators and prey • The life cycle of a mammal • The life cycle of an amphibian • The life cycle of an insect • The life cycle of a bird • All about reproduction • What is evolution? • Our changing environment

Electricity

- What is electricity? • Where does electricity come from? • What do we use electricity for? • All about static electricity • Electrical current and circuits • Conductors and insulators • All about batteries • Electricity and magnetism • How do we make electricity? • All about renewable energy • How do we measure electricity? • Powering circuits

Rocks

- What are Rocks? • All about our rocky planet • What are igneous rocks? • What are sedimentary rocks? • What are metamorphic rocks? • All about the rock cycle • All about erosion and weathering • What are the properties of rocks? • All about fossils • All about soil • What are precious stones? • Amazing rocks

Forces

- What is a force? • Forces around us • What is gravity? • What is magnetism? • All about friction • What is air resistance? • What is water resistance? • All about upthrust • All about elasticity • Balanced and unbalanced forces • All about pressure • Making forces bigger

Sound

- What is sound? • Sound on the move • Loud and soft • Sound and hearing • What is an echo? • Blocking sound • Ultrasound and infrasound • Animal hearing • What is music? • Recording sounds • Sound and science

Light

- What is light? • Sources of light • Light on the move • Light and materials • What are shadows? • What is reflection? • What is refraction? • Colourful light • Light and sight • Light and life • Types of light • Light and health

States of Matter

- Materials and matter • States of matter • All about solids • All about liquids • All about gases • Melting and freezing • Evaporating, boiling and condensing • The water cycle • What is a mixture? • Separating mixtures • Permanent state changes • The future of materials